Russian Step By Step

Natasha Alexandrova

Reading Russian

Illustrations by Elena Litnevskaya

Cover by Elena Litnevskaya

Technical Director Vsevolod Tsurikov

Workbook

Total Beginner

russianstepbystep.com

Fifth Edition
Reading Russian Workbook Russian Step By Step

All rights reserved

Copyright © 2009 by Russian Step By Step

ISBN-13: 978-0-9823042-1-1

ISBN-10: 0-9823042-1-8

Printed in the United States of America

Table of Contents

Introduction

Russian is spoken on a vast territory of the former Soviet Union.

Whether you are a serious learner or just want to be able to read street signs, menus or maps while in Russia, 'Reading Russian' Workbook from the 'Russian Step By Step' series can help you with that.

There are only 6 lessons, so, if you study 2 hours a day, you will be able to read Russian in a week.

The book has a lot of writing activities. Please, do all of them without skipping any part. When you write, your eye, your hand and your brain work together, filling out a special cell in your brain. Remember: the more you learn now the easier it will be for you to learn more complicated stuff. At least the reading part won't take much of your time.

The activities are accompanied by audio tracks ┃ **T1** ┃ - this sign stands for the audio track, which gives you understanding of the correct pronunciation and helps to build up confidence.

Upon completion of this book you will be able to read in Russian and will learn how to form positive and negative statements, yes/no questions, general (who, what, where) questions and you will also learn about genders of Russian nouns.

Good luck!

Free Audio Component

After purchasing the book, download your FREE audio component **right away!**
Listening is a crucial step to establish the correct pronunciation.

- ❖ To **ACCESS** your **FREE Direct Download**, please **REGISTER** on the russianstepbystep.com website.

- ❖ After registration you will receive an email to **verify** that your email address is correct. Press the verification link in the email and **you are ready to listen**! On the website you will see that **your status** (in the upper menu next to your name) changes to **Student RR**.

- ❖ **GO TO Audio for Workbook Reading Russian** and **listen** the audio Tracks right there or **download** them onto your computer.

- ❖ Please visit the Help page on our website if you have problems.

NOTE. If you would like **to purchase the audio CD** (exactly the same content as on the FREE Direct Download), please visit **the Store page** on our website russianstepbystep.com

Cyrillic Alphabet

Even though the Cyrillic alphabet looks different from the Roman one, it is pretty easy to learn it.

In the Russian Alphabet, like in many others, letters have their names and the corresponding sounds.

Reading in Russian is really easy in comparison to English. There are certain rules for reading, and, if you know them, you are able to read any word.

For example in English it is impossible for a foreigner to read the words: blood, poor, and floor correctly, if you do not know the pronunciation. It does not happen in Russian.

So, in order to be able to read Russian, you have to learn the sounds that the Russian letters make together with the rules. In this book only very basic rules are given. If you want to learn more, Russian Step By Step Beginner 1 book can help you. It has a special section (Pre-course) at the beginning of the book.

Read the alphabet trying to understand how the letters are pronounced. Concentrate on the sounds (see transliteration column).

Some of the letters are really easy, because they look very similar to the English ones and make similar sounds: A, O, T, E, K, and C.

Some of them look different, but make similar sounds: Б, Г, Д, Ё, Ч, Ж, И.

Some of them look different and are pronounced differently: Щ, Ы, Ц.

And some of them look similar, but make different sounds: Р, Н, В, Х.

 Those are the tricky ones.

But, if you learn them slowly step by step, they won't trick you later on. So, if you see a Russian word, you have a certain expectation of pronunciation.

In this book Russian letters are introduced not in the alphabetical order.

All Russian words in Russian Step By Step books are given with a stress mark. Knowing which vowel is stressed in the word is very important, because it affects pronunciation.

Russian Alphabet

Read the alphabet once, then listen to the audio (Track1) and repeat after the native speaker.

Printed Letter	Script	Name in the Alphabet	Transliteration of the Sound	Similar English Sound
А а	*Аа*	а	[a]	like **a** in father
Б б	*Бб*	бэ	[b]	like **b** in book
В в	*Вв*	вэ	[v]	like **v** in vet
Г г	*Гг*	гэ	[g]	like **g** in goose
Д д	*Дд*	дэ	[d]	like **d** in drama
Е е	*Ее*	е	[ye]	like **ye** in yet
Ё ё	*Ёё*	ё	[yo]	like **yo** in yoga
Ж ж	*Жж*	жэ	[ʒ]	like **su** in treasure
З з	*Зз*	зэ	[z]	like **z** in zebra
И и	*Ии*	и	[ee]	like **ee** in week
Й й	*Йй*	и краткое	[y]	like **y** in boy
К к	*Кк*	ка	[k]	like **k** in kitten
Л л	*Лл*	эль	[l]	like **l** in lamp
М м	*Мм*	эм	[m]	like **m** in man
Н н	*Нн*	эн	[n]	like **n** in note
О о	*Оо*	о	[o]	like **a** in ball
П п	*Пп*	пэ	[p]	like **p** in pet
Р р	*Рр*	эр	[r]	like **r** in red
С с	*Сс*	эс	[s]	like **s** in son

Printed Letter	Script	Name in the Alphabet	Transliteration of the Sound	Similar English Sound
Т т	*Тт*	тэ	[t]	like **t** in **t**oy
У у	*Уу*	у	[u]	like **oo** in gr**oo**m
Ф ф	*Фф*	эф	[f]	like **f** in **f**ly
Х х	*Хх*	ха	[h]	like **h** in **h**at
Ц ц	*Цц*	цэ	[ts]	like **ts** in boo**ts**
Ч ч	*Чч*	чэ	[ch]	like **ch** in **ch**air
Ш ш	*Шш*	ша	[sh]	like **sh** in **sh**awl
Щ щ	*Щщ*	ща	[shsh]	like **shsh** in English **sh**ip
Ъ	*ъ*	твёрдый знак	-	*
ы	*ы*	ы	[i]	like **i** in s**i**t
ь	*ь*	мягкий знак	-	**
Э э	*Ээ*	э	[e]	like **a** in r**a**t
Ю ю	*Юю*	ю	[yu]	like **you** in **you**th
Я я	*Яя*	я	[ya]	like **ya** in **ya**rd

There are 33 letters in Russian alphabet: 10 vowels, 21 consonants and 2 silent letters – ь and ъ.

* Ъ — твёрдый знак = hard sign

** Ь – мягкий знак = soft sign

These 2 letters do the same job: they separate the vowel from the rest of the word.

The vowel following either of these two letters sounds exactly as in the alphabet.

Soft sign also does more: it softens the preceded consonant. You will learn about this in Lesson 5.

As you might have noticed, some Russian cursive letters look different from the printed ones. If you are willing to learn cursive, you can repeat all the exercises in this script upon completing them all in block letters.

Vowels

Let us talk a little bit about Russian vowels, because there are some special rules about them that are really important to know at the beginning.

There are 10 vowels in Russian alphabet and they can be divided into five pairs, because they make similar sounds.

Hard Vowels		Soft Vowels
А	⟶	Я [йа]
Э	⟶	Е [йе]
О	⟶	Ё [йо]
У	⟶	Ю [йю]
Ы	⟶	И

The first four pairs of vowels make really similar sounds: one is harder, another is softer. The soft vowel in each pair has two sounds: [й + hard vowel]. Listen to the audio track and feel the difference between hard and soft vowels.

As was mentioned in the Introduction stress affects pronunciation. All stressed vowels sound very similar to the alphabet. But there are 2 vowels which sound really different when not stressed: O and E:

When not stressed:

! **O** sounds as **A** !

E sounds as **И**

Very often Russian sounds are similar but not exactly the same as the English ones. There are more pronunciation rules in Russian, which are introduced in the next book Russian Step By Step, Beginner. The purpose of this book is to familiarize you with the most important basic ones. Listen to the audio and repeat after native speakers.

If you have any questions, you can go to the russianstepbystep.com website and post them on the forum. In certain regions of Russia people have slightly different accents. For example, in Volga river region, people always pronounce O as O (no matter whether it is stressed or unstressed).

However, the difference is not that big. It's like between American English and British English. They still understand each other.

Lesson 1

 Exercise 1

Reading in Russian is much easier than it might look.

In the 1st line of the box there are letters that look similar and make the sounds similar to the English ones.

> **А а, К к, М м, О о, С с, Т т**
>
> **П п, Л л**

In the second line of the box there are 2 letters - **П п** and **Л л** - that look different from the English letters, but sound like **P** in Paul and **L** lamp.

Try to read the following words, then listen to the audio and repeat after the native speaker. After that write the words down.

T 3

 па́па _____

 ма́ма _____

 кот _____

 стол _____

 ла́мпа _____

 сала́т _____

Э The letter **Э** is pronounced like **a** in rat.

Э́то ма́ска.
This is a mask.

Э́то ко́ка-ко́ла.
This is Coca-Cola.

Pay attention to the pronunciation of the letter **o** in the word **это**.

The letter **o** is pronounced as **a** when not stressed.

это = [эта]

Exercise 2

Create positive statements, following the example. Listen to the audio and repeat.

Example: 1. **Это мама.**

1. _____

2. _____

3. _____

4. _____

5. _____

6. _____

Д	The letter **д** is pronounced like **d** in **d**og.

- Это дом?
- *Is this a house?*

- Да, это дом.
- *Yes, this is a house.*

- Это молоко́?

- Да, э́то молоко́.

 Exercise 3

Create pairs of questions and answers about the following pictures as in the example.

Example: 1. **Это папа? Да, это папа.**

1.

_____

2.

_____

3.

_____

4.

_____

5.

_____

6.

_____

T 7

3, Е
Н,

The letter **3** is pronounced similar the English **Z**.

The letter **Е** looks like the English **E**. However, it is pronounced like **ye** in **ye**t.

The letter **Н** is a tricky one, because it looks familiar, but it is pronounced like **n** in **n**o.

The good thing about this letter is that you will memorize it easily, because it stands for Russian **нет** (no). So, you will use it a lot.

- Э́то молоко́?
- _Is this milk?_

- Нет, э́то не молоко́. Э́то но́та.
- _No, this is not milk. This is a note._

- Э́то ко́ка-ко́ла?
- Нет, э́то не ко́ка-ко́ла.

Э́то знак "Стоп".
This is a Stop sign.

Exercise 4

Answer the questions following the example.

Example: 1. **Нет, это не кока-кола. Это маска.**

1. Это кóка-кóла? _____

   _____

2. Это молокó? _____

   _____

3. Это дом? _____

   _____

4. Это кот? _____

   _____

5. Это салáт? _____

   _____

6. Это знак «Стоп»? _____

   _____

7. Это лáмпа? _____

   _____

8. Это мáска? _____

   _____

 **Exercise 5**

Translate into Russian.

1. This is a table. _____

2. This is Dad. This is Mom. _____

3. Is this a mask? No, this is not a mask. _____

4. This is a stop sign. _____

5. Is this is salad? No, this is not a salad. _____

6. Is this a note? No, this is not a note. _____

7. Is this a milk? Yes, this is a milk. _____

8. Is this a cat? Yes, this is a cat. _____

9. Is this Coca-Cola? No, this is not Coca-Cola. This is milk. _____

_____

The last exercise that comes in the end of each lesson is for comprehension. The sentences are pronounced at a natural speed. Make sure you understand them without looking at the script.

Lesson 2

These 3 letters look different, but make the sounds that exist in English.

Б, И, Ч

Б ———→ like **b** in **b**oy

И ———→ like **ee** in w**ee**k

Ч ———→ like **ch** in **ch**ange

- Это чемпио́н.

- Это кот?
- Нет, это не кот.
- Кто это?
- *Who is this?*
- Это соба́ка.

- Это ма́ска?
- Нет, это не ма́ска.
- Что это?
- *What is this?*
- Это диск.

Notice that the letter **ч** in the word **что** is pronounced like **sh in sh**awl. This is an exception.

что = [што]

 Exercise 6

Put questions to the following statements as in the example.

Example:

Кто это?

1. Это мама. _____

2. Это но́та. _____

3. Это па́па. _____

4. Это знак «Стоп». _____

5. Это сала́т. _____

6. Это пило́т. _____

7. Это молоко́. _____

8. Это А́нна. _____

9. Это ма́ска. _____

Или

T 10

- Э́то Том или Ли́нда?
- *Is this Tom or Linda?*

- Э́то Ли́нда.
- *This is Linda.*

- Это пчела́ и́ли соба́ка?
- *Is it a bee or a dog?*

- Это пчела́.
- *It is a bee.*

As you might notice, there are no articles in Russian: **пчела** means **a** bee or **the** bee.

Exercise 7

Answer 'or 'questions, following the example.

Example: **1. Это кот.**

1.   Это кот или собáка? _____

2.   Это мáска úли знак «Стоп»? _____

3.   Это нóта или чек? _____

4.   Это дом úли стадиóн? _____

5.   Это банáн или лимóн? _____

6.   Это банк или таксú? _____

Exercise 8

Read the following words, then listen to the audio and repeat after the native speaker.
Consult the dictionary, if you are not sure about the meaning.
Write the words down.

1. пе́пси-ко́ла **пепси-кола** _____

2. бале́т _____

3. анекдо́т _____

4. систе́ма _____

5. чемпио́н _____

6. мета́лл _____

7. дипло́м _____

8. капита́н _____

9. поли́тика _____

10. эконо́мика _____

| ф | The letter **ф** is pronounced like **f** in **f**ather.

Это фо́то.

Это сок.

- Это сок?
- *Is it juice?*

- Это не сок. Это ко́фе.
- *It's not juice. It's coffee.*

Exercise 9

Answer the questions, following the example.

Example: **1. Это не маска. Это диск.**

1.  Это ма́ска? _____

2.   Это ко́фе? _____

3.  Это о́фис? _____

4.   Это лимо́н? _____

5.   Это дипло́м? _____

T 14

 Exercise 10

Translate into Russian. Listen to the audio. The sentences are pronounced at natural speed.

1. This is a stadium. _____

2. This is not a note. _____

3. Is this a bank? No, this is an office. _____

_____

4. Is this Tom or Linda? This is Linda. _____

_____

5. Who is this? This is a champion. _____

_____

6. What is this? This is a metal. _____

_____

7. Is this a cat or a dog? This is a dog. _____

_____

8. Who is this? This is a captain. _____

_____

9. Is this a salad? Yes, this is a salad. _____

_____

Lesson 3

| **Г, В** | The letter **Г** looks different, but is pronounced like **g** in **g**ame.

The letter **В** can be confusing at the beginning, because it is pronounced like **v** in **v**an. |

- Кто это?
- Who is this?

Это челове́к.
-This is a human being.

- Что это?
- What is this?

- Это кни́га.
- This is a book.

- А что это тако́е?
- And what is this?

- Это ва́за.
- This is a vase.

Что это? = Что это такое? These two questions are translated into English equally. The word **такое** just adds more curiosity.

Кто means who and stands for all alive creatures: people, animals, birds, ect.
Что means what and stands for all inanimate objects.

 Exercise 11

Ask questions about animate and inanimate objects and answer them following the example.

Example: **1. Что это такое? Это банан.**

2. Кто это? Это человек.

1. _____

2. _____

3. _____

4. _____

5. _____

6. _____

7. _____

8. _____

9. _____

| **Я** | The letter **Я** is pronounced like **ya** in **yar**d. | **T 16** |

Я Светла́на.
I am Svetlana.

Я Ива́н.

Я Мо́ника.

Я Ви́лли.
I am Willy.

Я Ли́нда.

| **Р** | The closest sound in English to the Russian letter **Р** is **r** in **r**un. |

But, of course it's not the same. Just listen to the native speaker and repeat it a lot of times.
Don't worry if you don't reproduce it correctly for the first time. Everything comes with practice.

- Это балери́на или до́ктор?
- is this a ballerina or a doctor?

- Это балери́на.
- This is a ballerina.

- Это крокоди́л или зе́бра?
 - Is this a crocodile or zebra?

- Это зе́бра.
- This is a zebra.

24

Exercise 12

Read the following words, then listen to the audio and repeat after the native speaker.
Consult the dictionary if you need help with translation. Write the words down.

1. метро́ __метро_____

2. фи́рма _____

3. спортсме́н _____

4. актри́са _____

5. Ро́берт _____

6. сигаре́та _____

7. Мари́я _____

8. па́спорт _____

9. дире́ктор _____

10. класс _____

11. бизнесме́н _____

12. Аме́рика _____

13. рестора́н _____

14. Калифо́рния _____

Это/то

Э́то я́блоко.
This is an apple.

То мандари́н.
That is a mandarin.

- Что э́то?   - Э́то очки́.
- *What is this?*   - *These are glasses.*

- Что то?   - То стака́н.
- *What is that?*   - *That is a glass.*

25

Exercise 13

Create pairs of statements about close and remote objects.

Example: **1. Кто это? Это пчела.**
            Кто то? То кот.

1.

_____

_____

2. _____

_____

3. _____

_____

4. _____

_____

5. _____

_____

6. _____

_____

Exercise 14

Answer the questions, following the example.

Example: **1. Нет, это не доктор. Это балерина.**

1. Это до́ктор? _____

_____

2. Это зе́бра? _____

_____

3.   Это я́блоко? _____

_____

4. Это стака́н? _____

_____

5. Это ко́фе? _____

_____

6. Это пчела́? _____

_____

Exercise 15

Translate into Russian.

1. This is a passport. _____

2. Is this an athlete? Yes, this is an athlete. _____

_____

3. This is an apple. That is a mandarin. _____

_____

4. Who is that? That is a doctor. _____

5. Who is this? This is a human being. _____

_____

6. What is that? Those are glasses. _____

7. Is this a cigarette? Yes, this is a cigarette. _____

_____

8. This is the crocodile. _____

9. I am not Maria. I am Monica. _____

Lesson 4

Ж, У

These two letters look unfamiliar for an English speaker.
They are pronounced like:

Ж ⟶ like **su** in trea**s**ure   **У** ⟶ like **oo** in gr**oo**m

Ж-ж-ж-ж....

Это муж, а э́то жена́.
This is a husband and this is a wife.

Э́то жук, и э́то то́же жук.
This is a beetle and this is also a beetle.

Notice how the conjunctions **а** and **и** join the sentences.

When we list different things we use **а**.

When we list similar things we use **и**.

 ## Exercise 16

Write the statements about the following pictures, using the proper conjunctions **а** or **и**.

Example: **1. Это нота, а это маска.**

2. Это кот, и это тоже кот.

1.

2.

3.

4.

5.

6.

7.

8.

9.

| Ё | The letter **Ё** is pronounced like **yo** in **yo**gurt. | T 22 |

It is not difficult to memorize Ё, because this is the only letter that has two dots above.
Letter Ё is always stressed.

ёж

a hedgehog

ёлка

a pine tree

Это пилот, а то самолёт.

This is a pilot, and that is an airplane.

If you listen carefully to the audio, you might notice that the letter **Ж** in the word 'ёж' is pronounced as **Ш**. Similar things happen in English too. Think about the '**ed**' ending in the words 'washed' and 'learned':

wash**ed** - you hear **t**   learn**ed** - you hear **d**

Generally, in Russian only the stressed syllable is pronounced articulately.

 Exercise 17   T 23

Read the following words, then listen to the audio and repeat after the native speaker.
Consult the dictionary if you need help with translation. Write the words down.

1. бокс **бокс** _____

2. ви́ски _____

3. платфо́рма _____

4. актёр _____

5. сувени́р _____

6. пинг-понг _____

7. парк _____

8. футбо́л _____

9. зоопа́рк _____

10. гимна́стика _____

11. сигна́л _____

12. гара́ж _____

13. лимона́д _____

14. жира́ф _____

Й The letter **Й** is pronounced like **y** in bo**y**.

Russian word **мой** means **my**.

Это мой стул.
This is my chair.

Это мой чай.
This is my tea.

Это мой ме́неджер.
This is my manager.

Many Russian male names have **й** in the end.

Никола́й, Андре́й, Алексе́й, Григо́рий, Матве́й.

Exercise 18

Pretend all the following objects are yours. Write statements about that.

Example: **1. Это мой дом.**

1. _____

2. _____

3. _____

4. _____

5. _____

6. _____

7. _____

Exercise 19

Usually all foreign names sound a little bit different from their origin. Listen to the audio, repeat after the native speaker and try to write American names in Russian.

1. John **Джон** _____

2. Joanne _____

3. Jimmy _____

4. Julia _____

5. Bob _____

6. Nancy _____

7. Frank _____

8. Debra _____

9. Kevin _____

10. Mary _____

11. Mike _____

12. Laura _____

13. Greg _____

14. Jennifer _____

15. Joe _____

16. Patricia _____

17. Richard _____

18. Barbara _____

19. Jason _____

20. Margaret _____

Exercise 20

Translate into Russian.

T 27

1. This is a husband and this is a wife. _____

2. This a bee and this is also a bee. _____

3. Is it a beetle? Yes, it's a beetle. _____

4. Who is this? This is my manager. _____

_____

5. What is this? This is my souvenir. _____

_____

6. Is this a table? No, this is not a table. What is this? This is a chair. _____

_____

7. Is this is a hedgehog? Yes, this is a hedgehog._____

_____

8. Is this a fir-tree? No, this is not a fir-tree. _____

_____

9. Is it a house or an office? It's a house. _____

_____

10. This is not my tea. That is my tea. _____

_____

11. I am not Robert. I am Richard. _____

_____

12. What is that? That is tea. _____

13. Is that a mandarin? No, that is an apple. _____

_____

Lesson 5

| **Х, Ц** | The letter **Х** is another tricky one. It is pronounced very similar to **h** in **h**at.

The letter **Ц** looks different but is pronounced exactly like **ts** in boo**ts**. | **T 28** |

хлеб пи́цца Хо́лодно!
It's cold!

T 29

Exercise 21

Read the following words, then listen to the audio and repeat after the native speaker.
Consult the dictionary if you need help with translation. Write the words down.

1. кио́ск **киоск**

2. хокке́й _____

3. аэропо́рт _____

4. пеницилли́н _____

5. бадминто́н _____

6. информа́ция _____

7. ре́гби _____

8. администра́ция _____

9. ко́смос _____

10. музе́й _____

11. поли́ция _____

12. суп _____

Exercise 22

Answer the questions following the example.

Example: **1. Нет, это не ресторан. Это кафе.**

1. Это рестора́н? _____

   _____

2. Это жук? _____

3. Это хлеб? _____

   _____

4. Это очки́? _____

   _____

5. Это пеницилли́н? _____

   _____

6. Это кио́ск? _____

   _____

7. Это крокоди́л? _____

   _____

ь, ъ These two letters are silent letters.

ь - soft sign has 2 main functions

1) works as a separation sign, when it is followed by a vowel;

семья́ — family   жильё — habitation

2) softens the preceding consonant;

мать — mother   контро́ль — control   конь — horse

In order to feel what difference the soft sign makes, listen to the pairs of words with soft sign and without it:

семья́ — семя́   жильё — жилё

конь — кон   контро́ль — контро́л   фильм - филм

ъ – hard sign works as a separation sign in the same way as a soft sign. (In ancient times **ъ** was used a lot, but now it is used very rarely. There are not that many words with hard sign)

въезд – entrance (for the cars)   объём - volume   подъём — elevation

Gender of Nouns

All Russian nouns can be divided into 3 groups, depending on their gender: masculine, feminine and neuter. In the majority of the cases you can tell the gender of the word by its ending.

 - он: стол, музе́й, конь —   masculine nouns end in a consonant or in the soft sign;

 - она: мама, А́нглия, ёлка, мать —   feminine nouns end in **а** or **я** or in the soft sign;

 - оно: кафе́, я́блоко —   neuter nouns end in **о** or **е**.

As you see those nouns, that end in soft sign, can be either masculine or feminine. In this case you can find out the gender from the dictionary.

And, of course there are exceptions:

'папа' is, obviously, a masculine word.

- Где пу́дель?
- *Where is a poodle?*
 - Вот он.
- *Here he is.*

- Где меда́ль?
- *Where is the medal?*
 - Вот она́.
- *Here it is.*

- Где окно́?
- *Where is the window?*
 - Вот оно́.
- *Here it is.*

 Exercise 23

Divide the following words into three columns depending on the gender.

Ма́ма, па́па, челове́к, ва́за, ко́фе, кни́га, мета́лл, окно́, пчела́, соба́ка, чемпио́н, Ви́лли, я́блоко, Са́ра, балери́на, кафе́, такси́, контро́ль, меда́ль, метро́, музе́й, вино́, те́ннис, фо́то, зе́бра.

он	она	оно
	мама	

Exercise 24

Write pairs of questions and answers about the following pictures as in the example.

Example: **1. Где крокодил? Вот он.**

1. _____

2. _____

3. _____

4. _____

5. _____

6. _____

7. _____

8. _____

9. _____

10. _____

11. _____

12. _____

13. _____

14. _____

Exercise 25

Translate into Russian.

1. Is it cold? Yes, it is cold. _____

2. Is it bread or pizza? It is bread. _____

_____

3. This is not an office. This is a museum. _____

_____

4. This is soup and this is salad. _____

5. Is he a director? Yes, he is a director. _____

_____

6. Where is the manager? Here he is. _____

_____

7. Where is a taxi? Here it is._____

8. Where is the medal? Here it is. _____

_____

9. I am John and she is Julia. _____

10. He is Nikolay and he is also Nikolay._____

_____

11. Where is the entrance (for the cars)? Here it is. _____

_____

Lesson 6

T 35

Ш, Щ The letter **Ш** is pronounced as to **sh** in **sh**awl.

Это ба́бушка.
This is grandma.

Это де́душка.
This is grandpa.

Это щено́к.
This is a puppy.

The letter **Щ** looks similar to Ш, but has a little leg and is pronounced as **shsh** in Engli**sh sh**ip.

борщ = *Russian beetroot soup*   вещь = *thing*   щено́к = *puppy*

Generally **Щ** is pronounced softer then **Ш**. Listen to pairs of syllables with different vowels and compare the sounds:

T 36

ша – ща   шу- щу   шё – щё   ше- ще

T 37

Exercise 26

Read the following words, then listen to the audio and repeat after the native speaker.
Consult the dictionary if you need help with translation. Write the words down.

1. Чика́го **Чикаго** _____   2. Вашингто́н _____

3. пу́дель _____   4. шокола́д _____

5. транспорт _____ 6. Шéрон _____

7. шик _____ 8. секретáрша _____

9. диалóг _____ 10. теáтр _____

11. Натáша _____ 12. диáгноз _____

Exercise 27

Create shot dialogues following the example.

Example: **1. Это ёлка?**

Нет, это не ёлка.

Кто это?

Это жираф.

1. Это ёлка? _____

_____

2. Это шоколáд? _____

_____

3. Это щенóк? _____

_____

4. Это пýдель? _____

_____

5.  Это секрета́рша? _____

_____

6. Это борщ? _____

_____

7. Это музе́й? _____

_____

| Ы, Ю |

The letter **Ы** is pronounced similar to **i** in l**i**ve.

The letter **Ы** is often confused with **И**. Listen to the pairs of syllables with different consonants and compare the sounds:

| T 38 |

Ы-И   мы –ми   вы – ви   ры -ри   ны – ни   ты – ти

| T 39 |

Я Светла́на. Вы Ви́лли.
I am Svetlana. You are Willy.

Он Ива́н. Она Мо́ника.
He is Ivan. She is Monica.

43

рыба
fish

цветы́
flowers

сыр
cheese

T 40

Letter **Ю** is the last one. It looks unusual, but pronounced exactly as **you** in you.

T 41

Нью Йо́рк   Ю́лия   Ю́рий

T 42

Exercise 28

Read the following words, then listen to the audio and repeat after the native speaker.
Consult the dictionary if you need help with translation. Write the words down.

1. Нью-Джéрси **Нью-Джерси** _____

2. никоти́н _____

3. журна́л _____

4. мини́стр _____

5. нюа́нс _____

6. парла́мент _____

7. визи́т _____

8. бар _____

9. мира́ж _____

10. инструме́нт _____

11. саксофо́н _____

12. бриз _____

13. туалéт _____

14. клуб _____

Exercise 29

Answer the following questions as in the example.

Example: **1. Нет, это не пчела. Это пудель.**

1.   Это пчела́? _____

_____

2.   Это цветы́? _____

_____

3. Это хлеб? _____

_____

4.   Это ба́бушка? _____

_____

5.   Это ёлка? _____

_____

6.   Это стул? _____

_____

7. Это борщ? _____

_____

Exercise 30

Translate into Russian.

1. Where is Grandma? Here she is. _____

_____

2. Where is cheese? Here it is. _____

3. Where is the puppy? Here it is. _____

4. Is this beetroot soup or soup? This is beetroot soup. _____

_____

5. This is my manager. _____

_____

6. I am Sharon. You are Jack. He is Victor. She is Maria. _____

_____

7. Who is this? This is my grandpa. _____

8. Who is that? That is my dad. _____

_____

9. This is a bank and that is a café. _____

10. This is an office and that is also an office. _____

_____

11. Who are you? I am Svetlana. _____

12. This is not a Pepsi-Cola. This is Coca- Cola. _____

_____

Answer Key

Exercise 3

2. Это лампа? Да, это лампа. 3. Это стол? Да, это стол. 4. Это маска? Да, это маска.
5. Это салат? Да, это салат. 6. Это молоко? Да, это молоко.

Exercise 4

2. Нет, это не молоко. Это лампа. 3. Нет, это не дом. Это стол. 4. Нет, это не кот.
Это дом. 5. Нет, это не салат. Это кока-кола. 6. Нет, это не знак «Стоп». Это молоко.
7. Нет, это не лампа. Это нота. 8. Нет, это не маска. Это знак «Стоп».

Exercise 5

1. Это стол. 2. Это папа. Это мама. 3. Это маска? Нет, это не маска. 4. Это знак
«Стоп». 5. Это салат? Нет, это не салат. 6. Это нота? Нет, это не нота. 7. Это
молоко? Да, это молоко. 8. Это кот? Да, это кот. 9. Это кока-кола? Нет, это не кока-
кола. Это молоко.

Exercise 6

2. Что это? 3. Кто это? 4. Что это? 5. Что это? 6. Кто это? 7. Что это?
8. Кто это? 9. Что это?

Exercise 7

2. Это знак «Стоп». 3. Это нота. 4. Это дом. 5. Это банан. 6. Это такси.

Exercise 9

2. Это не кофе. Это сок. 3. Это не офис. Это дом. 4. Это не лимон. Это банан. 5. Это
не диплом. Это фото.

Exercise 10

1. Это стадион. 2. Это не нота.   3. Это банк? Нет, это офис.   4. Это Том или Линда? Это Линда. 5. Кто это? Это чемпион. 6. Что это? Это металл. 7. Это кот или собака? Это собака. 8. Кто это? Это капитан. 9. Это салат? Да, это салат.

Exercise 11

3. Что это такое? Это лимон.   4. Кто это? Это пчела. 5. Что это такое? Это кофе. 6. Что это такое? Это книга. 7. Что это такое? Это сок. 8. Кто это? Это собака. 9. Что это такое? Это фото.

Exercise 13

2. Что это? Это яблоко. Что то? То лимон.   3. Что это? Это ваза. Что то? То стакан. 4. Что это? Это очки. Что то? То книга. 5. Что это? Это фото. Что то? То кофе. 6. Кто это? Это зебра. Кто то? То собака.

Exercise 14

2. Нет, это не зебра. Это пчела. 3. Нет, это не яблоко. Это мандарин.   4. Нет, это не стакан. Это сигарета. 5. Нет, это не кофе. Это сок. 6. Нет, это не пчела. Это человек.

Exercise 15

1. Это паспорт. 2. Это спортсмен? Да, это спортсмен.   3. Это яблоко. То мандарин. 4. Кто то? То доктор.   5. Кто это? Это человек.   6. Что то? То очки. 7. Это сигарета? Да, это сигарета. 8. Это крокодил. 9. Я не Мария, я Моника.

Exercise 16

3. Это стол, и это тоже стол. 4. Это лимон, а это банан. 5. Это ваза, и это тоже ваза. 6. Это диск, а это сигарета. 7. Это пчела, а это жук. 8. Это лампа, и это тоже лампа. 9. Это человек, а это собака.

Exercise 18

2. Это мой крокодил.   3. Это мой мандарин. 4. Это мой стакан. 5. Это мой ёж. 6. Это мой чай. 7. Это мой кофе.

Exercise 19

2. Джоан 3. Джимми 4. Джулия 5. Боб 6. Нэнси 7. Фрэнк 8. Дебора 9. Кевин 10. Мэри 11. Майк 12. Лаура 13. Грэг 14. Дженифер 15. Джо 16. Патрисия 17. Ричард 18. Барбара 19. Джейсон 20. Маргарет.

Exercise 20

1. Это муж, а это жена. 2. Это пчела, и это тоже пчела. 3. Это жук? Да, это жук. 4. Кто это? Это мой менеджер. 5. Что это? Это мой сувенир. 6. Это стол? Нет, это не стол. Что это? Это стул. 7. Это ёж? Да, это ёж. 8. Это ёлка? Нет, это не ёлка. 9. Это дом или офис? Это дом. 10. Это не мой чай. То мой чай. 11. Я не Роберт. Я Ричард. 12. Что то (такое)? То чай. 13. То мандарин? Нет, то яблоко.

Exercise 22

2. Нет, это не жук. Это ёж. 3. Нет, это не хлеб. Это яблоко. 4. Нет, это не очки. Это ёлка. 5. Нет, это не пенициллин. Это пицца. 6. Нет, это не киоск. Это стул. 7. Нет, это не крокодил. Это жираф.

Exercise 23

Он: папа, человек, кофе, металл, чемпион, Вилли, контроль, музей, теннис.

Она: мама, ваза, книга, пчела, собака, Сара, балерина, медаль, зебра.

Оно: окно, яблоко, кафе, такси, метро, вино, фото.

Exercise 24

2. Где мандарин? Вот он. 3. Где кофе? Вот он. 4. Где хлеб? Вот он. 5. Где пицца? Вот она. 6. Где такси? Вот оно. 7. Где стул? Вот он. 8. Где чай? Вот он. 9. Где кафе? Вот оно. 10. Где ёж? Вот он. 11. Где ёлка? Вот она. 12. Где яблоко? Вот оно. 13. Где жираф? Вот он. 14. Где зебра? Вот она.

Exercise 25

1. Холодно? Да, холодно. 2. Это хлеб или пицца? Это хлеб. 3. Это не офис. Это музей. 4. Это суп, а это салат. 5. Он директор? Да, он директор. 6. Где менеджер? Вот он. 7. Где такси? Вот оно. 8. Где медаль? Вот она. 9. Я Джон, а она Джулия. 10. Он Николай, и он тоже Николай. 11. Где въезд? Вот он.

Exercise 27

2. Нет, это не шоколад. Что это? Это медаль. 3. Нет, это не щенок. Кто это? Это ёж. 4. Нет, это не пудель. Что это? Это пицца. 5. Нет, это не секретарша. Кто это? Это балерина. 6. Нет, это не борщ. Что это? Это книга. 7. Нет, это не музей. Что это? Это хлеб.

Exercise 29

2. Нет, это не цветы. Это рыба. 3. Нет, это не хлеб. Это сыр. 4. Нет, это не бабушка. Это дедушка. 5. Нет, это не ёлка. Это щенок. 6. Нет, это не стул. Это окно. 7. Нет, это не борщ. Это цветы.

Exercise 30

1. Где бабушка? Вот она. 2. Где сыр? Вот он. 3. Где щенок? Вот он. 4. Это борщ или суп? Это борщ. 5. Это мой менеджер. 6. Я Шерон. Вы Джек. Он Виктор. Она Мария. 7. Кто это? Это мой дедушка. 8. Кто то? То мой папа. 9. Это банк, а то кафе. 10. Это офис, и то тоже офис. 11. Вы кто? Я Светлана. 12. Это не пепси-кола. Это кока-кола.

Russian - English Dictionary

Every time a noun ends in a soft sign or has an irregular ending for the certain gender it is indicated by:

m - masculine   *f* – feminine   *n* - neuter

А

а and
администра́ция administration
актёр actor
актри́са actress
Аме́рика America
анекдо́т anecdote, funny story
аэропо́рт airport

Б

ба́бушка grandmother, granny
бадминто́н badminton
балери́на ballerina
бале́т ballet
бана́н banana
банк bank
бар bar
бизнесме́н businessman
бокс boxing
борщ beetroot soup
бриз breeze

В

ва́за vase
Вашингто́н Washington
визи́т visit
вино́ wine
ви́ски *n* whiskey
вот here
въезд entrance for vehicles

Г

гара́ж garage
где where
гимна́стика gymnastics

Д

да yes
де́душка grandfather, granddad
диа́гноз diagnosis
диало́г dialogue
дипло́м diploma
диск disk
дире́ктор director
дом house

Ё

ёж hedgehog
ёлка fir-tree

Ж

жена́ wife
жильё housing
жира́ф giraffe
жук beetle
журна́л magazine

З

зе́бра zebra
знак sign

зо́на zone, area
зоопа́рк zoo

И

и́ли or
информа́ция information
инструме́нт instrument

К

Калифо́рния California
капита́н captain
кафе́ café
кио́ск kiosk
класс class
клуб club
кни́га book
ко́ка – ко́ла Coca-Cola
контро́ль *m* control
конь *m* horse
ко́смос cosmos
кот cat
ко́фе *m* coffee
крокоди́л crocodile
кто who

Л

ла́мпа lamp
лимо́н lemon
лимона́д lemonade

М

ма́ма mom
мандари́н mandarin
ма́ска mask
мать *f* mother
меда́ль *f* medal
ме́неджер manager
мета́лл metal
метро́ metro

мини́стр minister
мира́ж mirage
мой my
молоко́ milk
муж husband
музе́й museum

Н

не not
нет no
никоти́н nicotine
но́та note
Нью-Дже́рси *n* New Jersey
Нью-Йорк New York
нюа́нс nuance

О

объём volume
окно́ window
он he
она́ she
оно́ it (neuter object)
о́фис office
очки́ glasses *(plural)*

П

па́па *m* dad
парк park
парла́мент parliament
па́спорт passport
пеницилли́н penicillin
пе́пси-ко́ла Pepsi-Cola
пило́т pilot
пинг-понг ping-pong
пи́цца pizza
платфо́рма platform
подъём elevation
поли́тика politics
поли́ция police
президе́нт president
при́нтер printer

пу́дель *m* poodle
пчела́ bee

Р

ре́гби *n* rugby
рестора́н restaurant
ры́ба fish

С

саксофо́н saxophone
сала́т salad
секрета́рша secretary
семья́ family
сигаре́та cigarette
сигна́л signal
систе́ма system
соба́ка dog
сок juice
спортсме́н athlete
стадио́н stadium
стака́н glass
стол table
стоп stop
стул chair
сувени́р souvenir
суп soup
сыр cheese

Т

такси́ *n* taxi
теа́тр theater
то that
то́же also
тра́нспорт transport
туале́т restroom, toilet
тури́ст tourist

Ф

фильм film
фи́рма firm

фо́то photo
футбо́л soccer

Х

хлеб bread
хокке́й hockey
хо́лодно cold

Ц

цветы́ flowers

Ч

чай tea
чек check
челове́к person, human being
чемпио́н champion
Чика́го Chicago
что what

Ш

шик chic
шокола́д chocolate

Щ

щено́к puppy

Э

эконо́мика economy
э́то this

Ю

Югосла́вия Yugoslavia

Я

я I
я́блоко apple

English-Russian Dictionary

A

actor   актёр
actress   актри́са
administration   администра́ция
airport   аэропо́рт
also   то́же
America   Аме́рика
and   а
anecdote   анекдо́т
apple   я́блоко
area   зо́на
athlete   спортсме́н

B

badminton   бадминто́н
ballerina   балери́на
ballet   бале́т
banana   бана́н
bank   банк
bar   бар
bee   пчела́
beetle   жук
beetroot soup   борщ
book   кни́га
boxing   бокс
bread   хлеб
breeze   бриз
businessman   бизнесме́н

C

café   кафе́
California   Калифо́рния
captain   капита́н

cat   кот
chair   стул
champion   чемпио́н
check   чек
cheese   сыр
Chicago   Чика́го
chic   шик
chocolate   шокола́д
cigarette   сигаре́та
class   класс
club   клуб
Coca-Cola   ко́ка – ко́ла
coffee *m* ко́фе
cold   хо́лодно
control *m* контро́ль
cosmos   ко́смос
crocodile   крокоди́л

D

dad *m* па́па
diagnosis   диа́гноз
dialogue   диало́г
diploma   дипло́м
director   дире́ктор
disk   диск
dog   соба́ка

E

economy   эконо́мика
elevation   подъём
entrance for vehicles   въезд

F

family   семья́

film **фильм**
fir-tree **ёлка**
firm **фи́рма**
fish **ры́ба**
flowers **цветы́**

G

garage **гара́ж**
giraffe **жира́ф**
glass **стака́н**
glasses **очки́**
grandfather *m* **де́душка**
grandmother **ба́бушка**
gymnastics **гимна́стика**

H

he **он**
hedgehog **ёж**
here **вот**
hockey **хокке́й**
horse *m* **конь**
house **дом**
housing **жильё**
human being **челове́к**
husband **муж**

I

I **я**
information **информа́ция**
instrument **инструме́нт**
it (neuter object) **оно́**

J

juice **сок**

K

kiosk **кио́ск**

L

lamp **ла́мпа**
lemon **лимо́н**
lemonade **лимона́д**

M

magazine **журна́л**
manager **ме́неджер**
mandarin **мандари́н**
mask **ма́ска**
medal *f* **меда́ль**
metal **мета́лл**
metro **метро́**
milk **молоко́**
minister **мини́стр**
mirage **мира́ж**
mom **ма́ма**
mother *f* **мать**
museum **музе́й**
my **мой**

N

New Jersey *n* **Нью-Дже́рси**
New York **Нью-Йорк**
nicotine **никоти́н**
no **нет**
not **не**
note **но́та**
nuance **нюа́нс**

O

office **о́фис**
or **и́ли**

P

park **парк**
parliament **парла́мент**
passport **па́спорт**
penicillin **пеницилли́н**

Pepsi-Cola **пе́пси-ко́ла**
person **челове́к**
photo **фо́то**
pilot **пило́т**
ping-pong **пинг-понг**
pizza **пи́цца**
platform **платфо́рма**
police **поли́ция**
politics **поли́тика**
poodle *m* **пу́дель**
president **президе́нт**
printer **при́нтер**
puppy **щено́к**

R

restaurant **рестора́н**
restroom **туале́т**
rugby *n* **ре́гби**

S

salad **сала́т**
saxophone **саксофо́н**
secretary **секрета́рша**
she **она́**
sign **знак**
signal **сигна́л**
soccer **футбо́л**
soup **суп**
souvenir **сувени́р**
stadium **стадио́н**
stop **стоп**
system **систе́ма**

T

table **стол**
taxi *n* **такси́**
tea **чай**
that **то**
theater **теа́тр**
this **э́то**
toilet **туале́т**
tourist **тури́ст**
transport **тра́нспорт**

V

vase **ва́за**
visit **визи́т**
volume **объём**

W

Washington **Вашингто́н**
what **что**
where **где**
whiskey *n* **ви́ски**
who **кто**
wife **жена́**
window **окно́**
wine **вино́**

Y

Yugoslavia **Югосла́вия**
yes **да**

Z

zebra **зе́бра**
zone **зо́на**
zoo **зоопа́рк**

Russian Step By Step learning system is designed by an experienced teacher and language course developers to introduce a step-by-step approach to learning Russian. Our goal is to provide the learners of Russian with clear and simple explanations and lots of practice.

For a complete list of titles, prices, more information about our company and learning materials, please, visit our website at **russianstepbystep.com**

If you are teaching Russian using our materials, you can contact us regarding a complimentary training at **info@russianstepbystep.com**

You can also follow us on Facebook: **facebook.com/RussianStepByStep**

Available Titles

Adult Learner's Series:

1. **Reading Russian Workbook**: Total Beginner (Book & Audio)
2. **Beginner** Level 1 (Book & Audio)
3. **Low Intermediate** Level 2 (Book & Audio)
4. **Intermediate** Level 3 (Book & Audio)
5. Russian Handwriting 1: **Propisi 1**
6. Russian Handwriting 2: **Propisi 2**
7. Russian Handwriting 3: **Propisi 3**
8. **Verbs of Motion**: Workbook 1
9. **Verbs of Motion**: Workbook 2

Children's Series:

1. Azbuka 1: **Coloring Russian Alhpabet:** Азбука- раскраска (Step 1)
2. Azbuka 2: **Playing with Russian Letters:** Занимательная азбука (Step2)
3. Azbuka 3: **Beginning with Syllables:** Мои первые слоги (Step 3)
4. Azbuka 4: **Continuing with Syllables**: Продолжаем изучать слоги (Step 4)
5. **Animal Names and Sounds**: Кто как говорит (Part 1 and Part 2)
6. **Animal Names and Sounds**: Кто как говорит (Part 1 and Part 2)
7. Propisi for Preschoolers 1: **Russian Letters: Trace and Learn:** Тренируем пальчики (Step 1)

34306980R00034

Made in the USA
Middletown, DE
16 August 2016